A Few of My Favorite

Miniature QUILTS

Christiane Meunier

D1063526

Moon over Mountain
2 Public Avenue,
Montrose, PA 18801-1220
www.QuiltTownUSA.com

Copyright ©2005 Moon Over Mountain

All Rights Reserved.
Published in the United States of America.
Printed in China.

Moon Over Mountain
2 Public Avenue
Montrose, Pennsylvania 18801-1220

No part of this publication may be reproduced or transmitted in any form or by any means, electronic or mechanical, including photocopy, recording, or any information storage and retrieval system now known or to be invented, without permission in writing from the publisher, except by a reviewer who wishes to quote brief passages in connection with a review written for inclusion in a magazine, newspaper, or broadcast.

First Printing: 2005

Library of Congress Cataloging-in-Publication Data
Meunier, Christiane, 1952-
A few of my favorite miniature quilts /
by Christiane Meunier.
   p. cm.
ISBN 1-885588-67-4 (pbk.)
1. Patchwork—Patterns. 2. Quilting—Patterns.
3. Miniature quilts. I. Title.
   TT835.M487215 2005
   746.46'041—dc22

                           2005010465

Design and Illustrations: Diane Albeck-Grick
Photography: Van Zandbergen Photography,
                  Brackney, Pennsylvania

Our Mission Statement
We publish quality quilting books that recognize, promote, and inspire self-expression. We are dedicated to serving our customers with respect, kindness, and efficiency.

www.QuiltTownUSA.com

Miniature Quilts

are a great way to become familiar with new techniques and to experiment with new color combinations without risking a lot of fabric or a lot of time. Working in a small scale is also a wonderful way to improve your accuracy. Beyond those marvelous reasons to make miniature quilts there is of course the end result.

Miniature quilts, like babies, let the soft non-judgmental part of yourself out. They are little art pieces that will turn your home into a treasure house where beauty flourishes on every wall. Quilts are cherished gifts that speak very tenderly and discreetly of your true feelings.

I chose these quilts because they embrace a combination of old and new that will make them a welcome addition to any décor. Then, of course, by changing the time period of the fabric, you can change their look to match your taste. Whatever the look, I know you will enjoy the delicate feminine touch that they will bring to your home.

With much love,

Christiane

Materials

- Fat quarter (18" x 20") each of blue, green, pink, and yellow
- 1/4 yard black
- 10" square of backing fabric
- 10" square of thin batting

Stained Glass K...

*Jill Majers of Troy, Montana, likes to see just how small she can go with her quilt designs. **"Stained Glass Kaleidoscope"** has twenty-three pieces in a mere 1 1/2" block. If you prefer a larger size, use the patterns on page 13.*

Cutting

Fabric for foundation piecing will be cut as you stitch the foundations. Each piece should be at least 1/4" larger on all sides than the section it will cover. Refer to the General Directions *as needed. All other dimensions include a 1/4" seam allowance.*

- Cut 5: 5/8" x 4 1/2" strips, black
- Cut 2: 5/8" x 2 1/2" strips, black
- Cut 1: 1 1/4" x 40" strip, black

Directions

Follow the foundation piecing instructions in the General Directions *to piece the blocks.*

1. Trace the full-size patterns on the foundation paper, transferring all lines and numbers. Make 4 each of Foundations A and B, and 2 each of Foundations C and D. Cut each one out on the outer line.

2. Piece each foundation in numerical order using the following fabrics in these positions:

For each Foundation A:

1 - yellow
2, 3 - black
4, 5 - blue
6, 7 - black
8, 9 - pink
10, 11 - black
12, 13 - blue
14, 15 - black
16, 17 - green
18, 19 - black
20, 21 - blue
22 - black
23 - blue

Trace this line for Foundation D

Trace this line for Foundation C

Trace this line for Foundation C

Trace this line for Foundation D

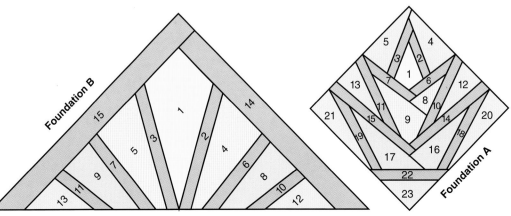

eidoscope

For each Foundation B:
- 1 - yellow
- 2, 3 - black
- 4, 5 - pink
- 6, 7 - black
- 8, 9 - green
- 10, 11 - black
- 12, 13 - blue
- 14, 15 - black

For each Foundation C and D:
- 1 - yellow
- 2, 3 - black
- 4, 5 - pink
- 6, 7 - black
- 8, 9 - green
- 10, 11 - black
- 12, 13 - blue

3. Trim the fabric 1/4" beyond the edges of each foundation.

Assembly

1. Stitch 2 Foundation A's to a 5/8" x 2 1/2" black strip. Make 2. Trim the excess from the ends of the black strips.

2. Stitch a 5/8" x 4 1/2" black strip between the units, carefully aligning the center blocks. Trim the excess from the black strip.

3. Stitch two 5/8" x 4 1/2" black strips to opposite sides of the unit. Trim the excess from the strips.

4. Stitch the remaining 5/8" x 4 1/2" black strips to the remaining sides and trim.

5. Center and stitch 2 Foundation B's to the sides of the unit.

6. Center and stitch the remaining Foundation B's to the remaining sides.

7. Stitch the Foundation C's to opposite sides of the quilt. Stitch the Foundation D's to the remaining sides.

8. Finish the quilt as described in the *General Directions*, using the 1 1/4" x 40" black strip for the binding.

Materials

NOTE: The quiltmaker used silk fabrics for this quilt, however cottons would also work well.

- Assorted bright scraps
- Fat eighth (10" x 18") cream
- Fat eighth black
- 17" square of backing fabric
- 17" square of thin batting
- Heavy paper

Tumbling Colors

Patricia Pinkus of Los Angeles, California, used the English Paper Piecing method to perfectly stitch this quilt. It's entirely hand pieced using silk fabrics and machine quilted. Patricia says the silk was a little more difficult to work with but the results made it worthwhile. ***"Tumbling Colors"*** *won a first place ribbon in the 2004 Miniatures from the Heart Contest.*

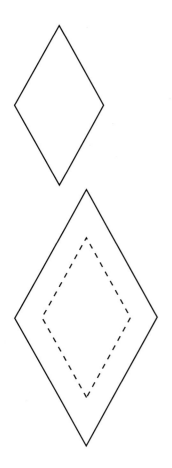

Cutting

The small diamond pattern is full size and does not include a seam allowance. The large diamond pattern includes a 1/4" seam allowance. All other dimensions include a 1/4" seam allowance.

- Cut 136 small diamonds from heavy paper
- Cut 42: large diamonds, brights
- Cut 42: large diamonds, black
- Cut 52: large diamonds, cream
- Cut 2: 1 3/4" x 35" strips, red, for the binding
- Cut 2: 2 3/4" x 16" strips, red
- Cut 2: 2 3/4" x 11" strips, red

Directions

1. Place a fabric diamond right side down on a flat surface. Center a paper diamond on top of the fabric piece. Fold the excess fabric neatly over the edge of the paper diamond and secure it with basting stitches. Baste all of the diamonds in this manner.

2. Lay out a bright diamond and a black diamond with the black one on the left. Place them right sides together and hand stitch them along one edge only, just catching the edge of the fabric.

3. Stitch a cream diamond to the unit in the same manner to make a block, as shown. Make 39.

4. Stitch a bright diamond to a cream diamond to make a left-edge unit. Make 3.

5. Stitch a black diamond to a cream diamond to make a right-

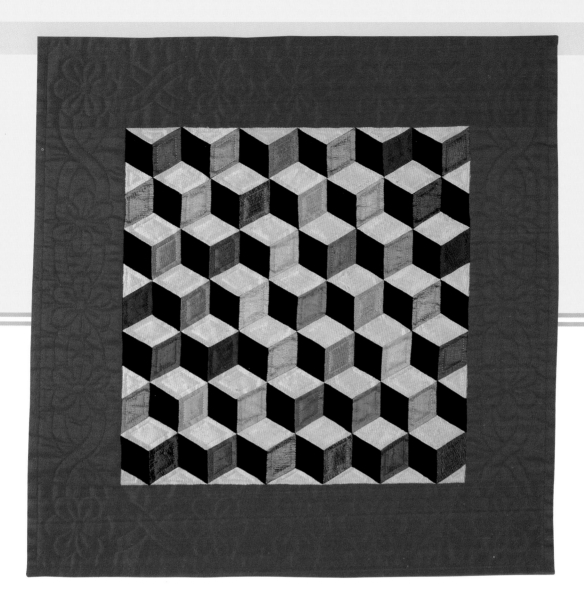

edge unit. Make 3.

6. Lay out the Tumbling blocks and edge units in 7 rows, as shown in the Assembly Diagram.

7. Stitch the units into rows. Join the rows.

8. Stitch the remaining cream diamonds to the bottom edge of the quilt.

9. Release the basting stitches on the diamonds around the edges of the quilt. Open the seam allowances and press them away from the quilt.

10. Trim the cream diamonds to straighten the edges, leaving a 1/4" seam allowance. Refer to the quilt as necessary.

11. Measure the length of the quilt. Trim the 2 3/4" x 11" red strips to that measurement. Sew them to the sides of the quilt.

12. Measure the width of the quilt, including the borders. Trim the 2 3/4" x 16" red strips to that measurement and stitch them to the top and bottom of the quilt.

13. Finish the quilt as described in the *General Directions*, using the 1 3/4" x 35" red strips for the binding.

Assembly Diagram

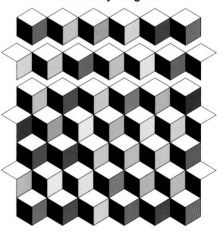

Materials

- 20 solid scraps, each at least 6" x 7"
- 1/2 yard green
- 23" x 26" piece of backing
- 23" x 26" piece of batting
- Variegated thread
- Fusible web

Whirligig #1

Anne Morrell-Robinson of Margaree Valley, Nova Scotia, Canada, is an award-winning quilter who also creates wearable art and hooked rugs. "Whirligigs #1" (20 1/2" x 23 1/2") is Anne's interpretation of a design she saw on some antique furniture. It's the first in a series of quilts she has made based on the whirligig.

Cutting

The whirligig pattern is full size and does not need a turn-under allowance. Trace the whirligig pattern on the paper side of the fusible web. Cut around the shape slightly beyond the drawn line. Following the manufacturer's directions, fuse the whirligig shapes to the wrong side of the appropriate fabric scraps. Cut them out on the drawn lines. All other dimensions include a 1/4" seam allowance.

- Cut 20: 3 1/2" squares, assorted solids
- Cut 20: whirligigs, assorted solids
- Cut 66: 1 1/2" squares, assorted solids, for the middle border
- Cut 2: 1 1/2" x 14 1/2" strips, green, for the inner border
- Cut 2: 1 1/2" x 15 1/2" strips, green, for the inner border
- Cut 4: 2 1/2" x 21" strips, green, for the outer border
- Cut 3: 1 1/4" x 40" strips, green, for the binding

Directions

1. Fold a 3 1/2" solid square in half twice and finger press the folds.
2. Place a whirligig on the square, using the creases for placement. Fuse the whirligig to the square. Make 20.
3. Using matching thread, topstitch each whirligig 1/16" to 1/8" from the edge.

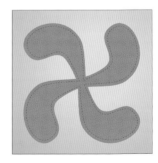

Assembly

1. Lay out the blocks in 5 rows of 4. Stitch the blocks into rows and join the rows.
2. Stitch the 1 1/2" x 15 1/2" green strips to the long sides of the quilt.
3. Stitch the 1 1/2" x 14 1/2" green strips to the remaining sides of the quilt.

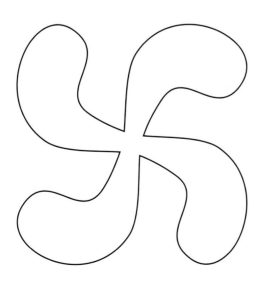

4. Stitch seventeen 1 1/2" assorted solid squares together to make a border strip. Make 2.

5. Stitch them to the sides of the quilt.

6. Stitch sixteen 1 1/2" assorted solid squares together to make a border strip. Make 2.

7. Stitch them to the top and bottom of the quilt.

8. Measure the length of the quilt through the center. Trim two 2 1/2" x 21" green strips to that measurement, and stitch them to the sides of the quilt.

9. Measure the width of the quilt through the center. Trim the remaining 2 1/2" x 21" green strips to that measurement, and stitch them to the remaining sides of the quilt.

10. Finish the quilt according to the *General Directions*, using the 1 1/4" green strips for the binding.

11. At the intersections of the blocks, satin stitch an "X" with variegated thread.

12. With 2 strands of thread, hand sew a button in the center of each whirligig block. Tie the ends, leaving 1/2"-long thread tails.

Materials

- Assorted lamé scraps
- Fat quarter (18" x 20") dark gray lamé
- Fat quarter plaid lamé
- 1/8 yard solid lamé for the piping
- Fat quarter stripe lamé for the binding
- 19" square of backing fabric
- 19" square of thin batting
- Paper for the foundations

Snail's Lamé

Scott Murkin of Asheboro, North Carolina, made **"Snail's Lamé"** *to use a bundle of lamé fabrics. Scott says he wanted to use all of the fabrics in a single quilt so he chose this foundation pieced, interlocking design, the Snail's Trail.*

Coloring Diagram

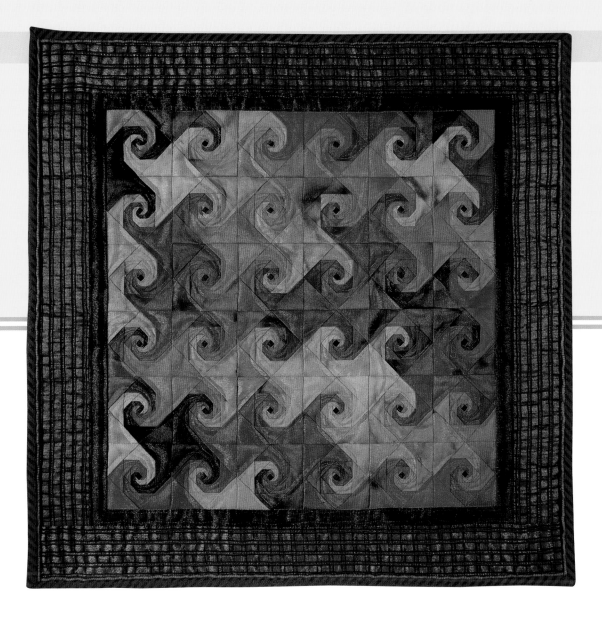

Cutting

Fabric for foundation piecing will be cut as you stitch the blocks. Each piece should be at least 1/4" larger on all sides than the section it will cover. Refer to the General Directions *as needed. All other dimensions include a 1/4" seam allowance.*

- Cut 4: 1" x 14" strips, dark gray
- Cut 2: 2" x 14" strips, plaid
- Cut 2: 2" x 17" strips, plaid
- Cut 4: 5/8" x 17" strips, solid lamé
- Cut 1 1/4"-wide bias strips, stripe lamé, to total at least 75" when joined for the binding

Preparation

1. Copy the coloring diagram on a copy machine. Make several copies in case you change your mind or make a mistake.

2. Using colored pencils in colors similar to your fabrics, color the diagram. Refer to the photo for guidance.

Directions

Follow the foundation piecing instructions in the General Directions *to piece the blocks.*

1. Trace the full-size pattern (page 12) 36 times on the foundation paper, transferring all lines. Cut each one out on the outer line.

2. Working from the colored diagram, piece the foundations using dark gray for the center square of each foundation. Begin piecing the first block using the colors in your diagram. To avoid confusion and aid in proper color placement, lightly color each foundation before you begin piecing it.

3. Piece each successive block, matching the colors with the blocks adjacent to it.

4. Trim the fabric 1/4" beyond the edges of each foundation.

5. Lay out each block as you

complete it. Make 36 blocks and lay them out in 6 rows of 6.

Assembly

1. Stitch the blocks into rows and join the rows.

2. Measure the width of the quilt. Trim two 1" x 14" dark gray strips to that measurement. Stitch them to opposite sides of the quilt.

3. Measure the length of the quilt, including the borders. Trim the remaining 1" x 14" dark gray strips to that measurement. Stitch them to the remaining sides of the quilt.

4. In the same manner, trim the 2" x 14" plaid strips to fit the quilt's width. Stitch them to oposite sides of the quilt.

5. Trim the 2" x 17" plaid strips to fit the quilt's length and stitch them to the remaining sides of the quilt.

6. Press the 5/8" x 17" solid lamé strips in half, right side out. Measure the width of the quilt. Trim the pressed strips to that measurement.

7. Baste 2 strips to opposite sides of the quilt, aligning the raw edges. Baste the remaining strips to the remaining sides.

8. Finish the quilt as described in the *General Directions*, using the 1 1/4"-wide stripe bias strips for the binding.

Foundation Pattern

Use this foundation for a bigger version

Make it Bigger!

For a larger version (26" square) of Snail's Lamé, use the following Materials and Cutting lists:

Materials

- Assorted lamé scraps
- 1/4 yard dark gray lamé
- 1/2 yard plaid lamé
- 1/8 yard solid lamé for the piping
- 1/4 yard stripe lamé for the binding
- 27" square of backing fabric
- 27" square of thin batting
- Paper for the foundations

Cutting

- Cut 4: 1 1/2" x 21" strips, dark gray
- Cut 2: 3 1/2" x 21" strips, plaid
- Cut 2: 3 1/2" x 25" strips, plaid
- Cut 4: 3/4" x 25" strips, solid lamé
- Cut 1 1/4"-wide bias strips, stripe lamé, to total at least 110" when joined for the binding

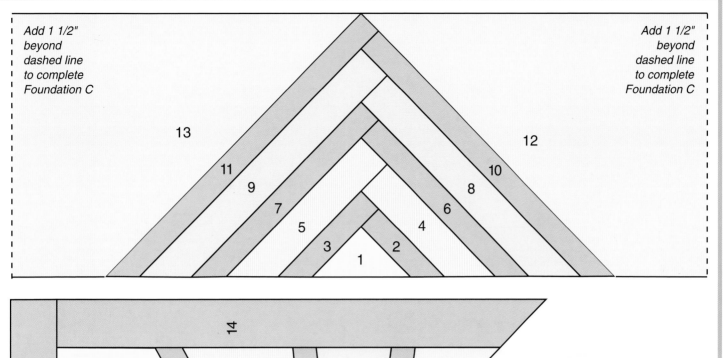

Add 1 1/2" beyond dashed line to complete Foundation C

Add 1 1/2" beyond dashed line to complete Foundation C

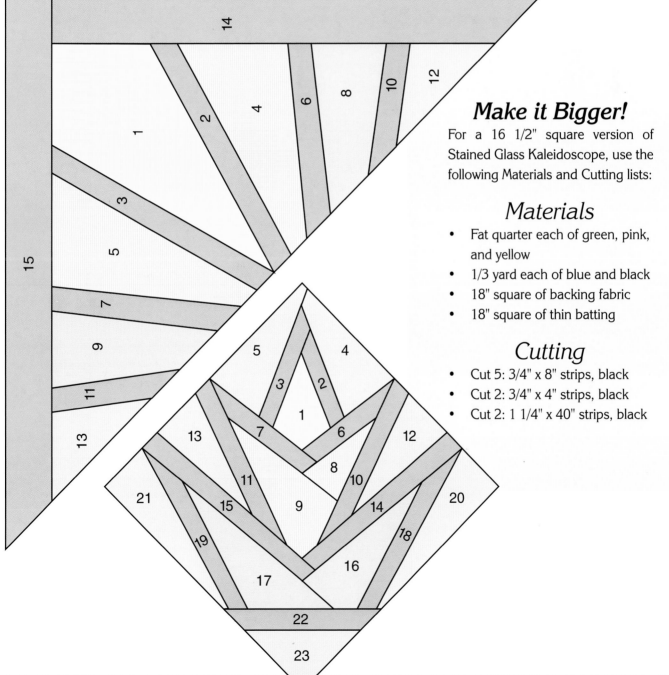

Make it Bigger!

For a 16 1/2" square version of Stained Glass Kaleidoscope, use the following Materials and Cutting lists:

Materials

- Fat quarter each of green, pink, and yellow
- 1/3 yard each of blue and black
- 18" square of backing fabric
- 18" square of thin batting

Cutting

- Cut 5: 3/4" x 8" strips, black
- Cut 2: 3/4" x 4" strips, black
- Cut 2: 1 1/4" x 40" strips, black

Piña Colada, California Style

*Jane Alameda of Lakeport, California, made this striking quilt with bright batiks and a Virginia Robertson black background print. Jane pieced "**Piña Colada, California Style**" on foundations.*

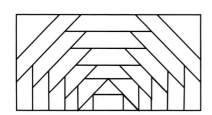

Cutting

Fabric for foundation piecing will be cut as you stitch the blocks. Each piece should be at least 1/4" larger on all sides than the section it will cover. Refer to the General Directions *as needed. All other dimensions include a 1/4" seam allowance.*

- Cut 4: 3/4" x 19" strips, bright green, for the inner border
- Cut 4: 2 1/2" x 19" strips, black, for the outer border
- Cut 2: 1 1/4" x 40" strips, black, for the binding
- Cut 8: 1 1/2" x 2 1/2" rectangles, black
- Cut 4: 1 1/2" squares, black

Directions

The foundation patterns are full size and do not include a seam allowance. Follow the foundation-piecing instructions in the General Directions *to piece the blocks.*

1. Trace the block pattern 25 times and the half block 12 times on the foundation paper, transferring all lines. Cut each foundation out on the outer line.

2. Piece each foundation using bright green, bright pink, and black as indicated in the colored diagrams.

3. Trim the fabric 1/4" beyond the edges of each foundation.

Materials

- 1/2 yard bright green
- 1/2 yard bright pink
- 5/8 yard black
- 19" square of backing fabric
- 19" square of thin batting

Half Block

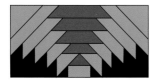

Make 12

Make 4

Make 4

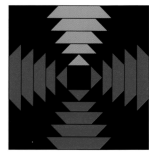

Make 4

Assembly

1. Referring to the photo, lay out the blocks, 1 1/2" x 2 1/2" black rectangles, and the 1 1/2" black squares. Stitch them into rows and join the rows.

2. Stitch a 3/4" x 19" bright green strip to a 2 1/2" x 19" black strip along their length to make a border. Make 4.

3. Center and stitch the borders to the sides of the quilt. Start, stop, and backstitch 1/4" from the ends.

4. Miter each corner.

5. Finish the quilt as described in the *General Directions*, using the 1 1/4" x 40" black strips for the binding.

Make 4

Make 4

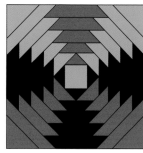

Make 4

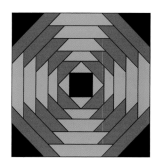

Make 1

Materials

- 144 print scraps, each at least 5" square
- Assorted print scraps, each at least 1 1/4" x 10", for the binding
- 39" square of backing fabric
- 39" squares of thin batting

Serendipity

Kathy Palmiter of Williams, Indiana, said **"Serendipity"** was a challenge in using her collection of fabric scraps. She arranged them beautifully from light to dark.

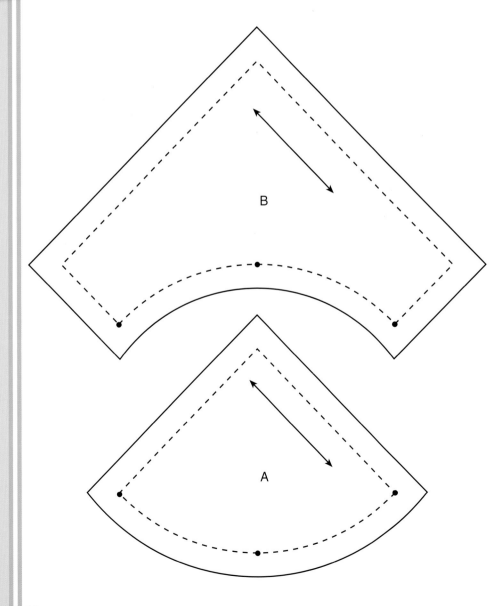

Cutting

The patterns are full size and include a 1/4" seam allowance, as do all dimensions given.

- Cut 144: A, assorted scraps
- Cut 144: B, assorted scraps

Also:

- Cut 16: 1 1/4" x 10" strips, assorted prints, for the binding

Directions

1. Referring to the photo, lay out the A's and B's in 12 rows of 12.

2. Working on one block at a time, pin the B to the A, matching the dots, as shown. Stitch the pieces together, aligning the edges as you go.

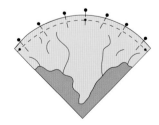

3. Press the seam allowance toward the A. Trim the seam allowance to 1/8". Place the block back in the

layout and piece the remaining blocks in the same manner.

Assembly

1. Stitch the blocks into rows and join the rows.

2. Lay the 1 1/4" x 10" strips next to the quilt to coordinate the values with the quilt.

3. Stitch the ends of the binding strips together with diagonal seams.

4. Finish the quilt as described in the *General Directions*, using the pieced strip for the binding.

Make it Smaller!

For a smaller version (18 1/2") of "Serendipity" use these pieces and your 2 1/2" scraps.

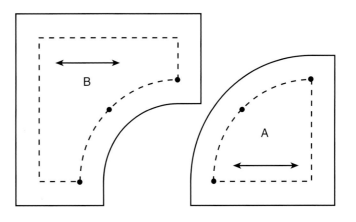

Materials

- Scraps of batiks and other prints in blue, purple, gray, green, black, tan, yellow, and pink
- 1/8 yard blue
- 1/2 yard variegated blue print
- 1/8 yard blue print for the binding
- 21" square of backing fabric
- 21" square of thin batting
- Paper for the foundations

Look for the Silver L

*Surprising sparks of yellow in this traditional Storm at Sea serve as a re-minder that we should always **"Look for the Silver Lining."** Pat Brady of Salem, Oregon, hand pieced the blocks on lightweight foundations then as-sembled them by machine. Pat says "This quilt is a well-seasoned traveler" as she worked on it while traveling by car, train, plane, and even cruise ship.*

Foundation A

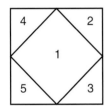

Foundation B

Foundation C

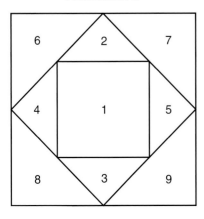

Cutting

Fabric for foundation piecing will be cut as you stitch the blocks. Each piece must be at least 1/2" larger on all sides than the section it will cover. Refer to the General Directions *as needed. All other dimensions include a 1/4" seam allowance.*

- Cut 64: 1" squares, assorted batiks and prints
- Cut 4: 3/4" x 14" strips, blue, for the inner border
- Cut 2: 2 3/4" x 15" strips, variegated blue print, with the pattern running across the strips (side borders)
- Cut 2: 2 3/4" x 19" strips, variegated blue print, with the pattern running the length of the strips (top and bottom borders)
- Cut 2: 1 1/4" x 40" strips, blue print, for the binding

Preparation

1. Stitch four 1" squares together to make a Four Patch. Make 16.

Directions

1. Trace the full-size patterns on the foundation paper, transferring all lines and numbers. Make 25 A's, 40 B's, and 16 C's.

2. Piece each foundation in num-erical order using the following fabrics in these positions:

For each foundation A:
    1 - light print
    2, 3, 4, 5 - dark prints

For each foundation B:
    1 - dark print
    2, 3, 4, 5 - light prints

For each foundation C:
    Four Patch, centered
    2, 3, 4, 5 - light prints
    6, 7, 8, 9 - dark prints

3. Trim the fabric 1/4" beyond the edges of each foundation.

Assembly

1. Referring to the photo, lay out the foundations in 9 rows of 9.

2. Stitch the foundations into rows. Join the rows.

3. Measure the length of the quilt. Trim 2 of the 3/4" x 14" blue strips to

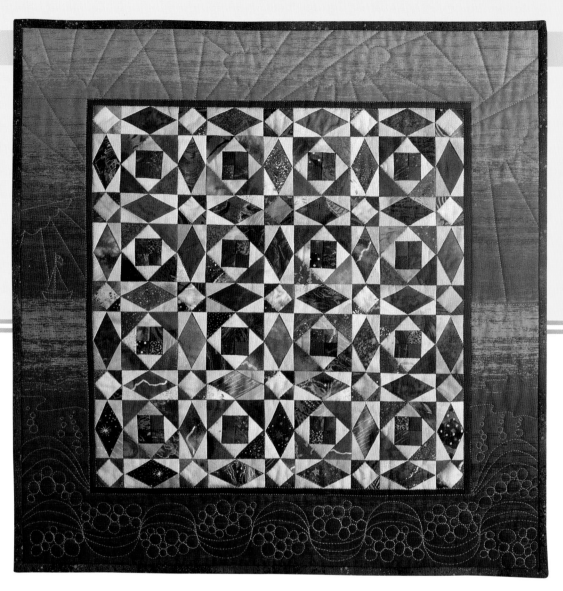

ining

that measurement. Stitch them to the sides of the quilt.

4. Measure the width of the quilt, including the borders. Trim the remaining 3/4" x 14" blue strips to that measurement. Stitch them to the top and bottom of the quilt.

5. In the same manner, trim the 2 3/4" x 15" variegated blue strips to fit the quilt's length. Stitch them to the sides of the quilt.

6. Trim the 2 3/4" x 19" variegated blue strips to fit the quilt's width and stitch them to the top and bottom of the quilt.

7. Finish the quilt as described in the *General Directions*, using the 1 1/4" x 40" blue print strips for the binding.

Quilting Designs

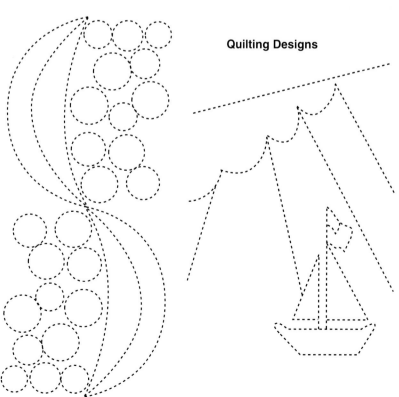

Materials

- Assorted bright hand-dyed scraps, each at least 5" square
- Fat quarter (18" x 20") bright hand-dyed fabric for the binding
- 1/2 yard black
- 20" square of backing fabric
- 20" square of thin batting
- Paper for the foundations

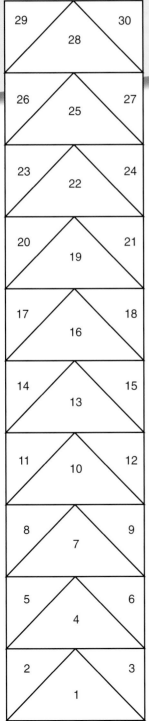

Glow

Barbara Engler of Bentonville, Arizona, named her quilt **"Glow"** because the hand-dyed fabrics seemed to glow when combined with black. To add to the look, Barbara used metallic thread for the quilting. This bright quilt won a third place ribbon in her guild's show.

Cutting

Fabric for foundation piecing will be cut as you piece the foundations. Each piece should be at least 1/4" larger on all sides than the section it will cover. Refer to the General Directions as needed. All other dimensions include a 1/4" seam allowance.

- Cut 4: 1 1/8" x 15" strips, black
- Cut 4: 2" x 9" strips, black
- Cut 4: 1 1/4" x 20" strips, bright fabric, for the binding

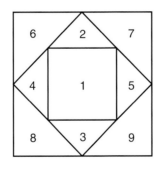

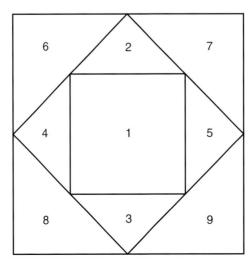

Directions

The foundation patterns are full size and do not include a seam allowance. Follow the foundation-piecing instructions in the General Directions to piece the blocks.

1. Trace the full size patterns on the foundation paper, transferring all lines and numbers. Cut each one out on the outer line. Make 25 large block foundations, 2 small block foundations, and 4 Flying Geese foundations.

2. Piece each foundation in numerical order using the following fabrics in these positions:

For one large block:
    1 - black
    2, 3, 4, 5 - one bright
    6, 7, 8, 9 - black
    10, 11, 12, 13 - same bright

For each of 24 large blocks and 4 small blocks:
    1 - bright

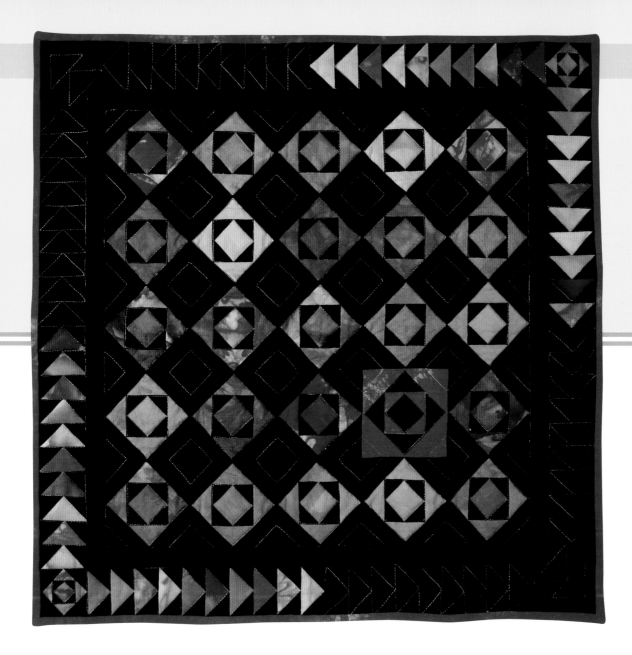

2, 3, 4, 5 - black

6, 7, 8, 9 - same bright

10, 11, 12, 13 - black

For each Flying Geese foundation:

Piece each Flying Geese foundation using assorted brights for the large triangles and black for the small triangles.

3. Trim the fabric 1/4" beyond the edges of each foundation.

Assembly

1. Referring to the photo, lay out the blocks in 5 rows of 5. Stitch the

blocks into rows and join the rows.

2. Measure the width of the quilt. Trim 2 of the 1 1/8" x 15" black strips to that measurement. Stitch them to opposite sides of the quilt.

3. Measure the length of the quilt. Trim the remaining 1 1/8" x 15" black strips to that measurement and stitch them to the remaining sides of the quilt.

4. Stitch a 2" x 9" black strip to the end of each Flying Geese section, as shown.

5. Trim 2 of the Flying Geese borders to fit the quilt's length, trimming only the black strip. Stitch the borders to the sides of the quilt.

6. Stitch the small blocks to the remaining Flying Geese borders. In the same manner, trim the borders to fit the quilt and stitch them to the remaining sides.

7. Finish the quilt as described in the *General Directions*, using the 1 1/4" x 20" bright strips for the binding.

Rainbow thru the Pines

*Inspired by an antique quilt, Jeanie Evans of Fort Smith, Arkansas, challenged herself to make **"Rainbow thru the Pines."** Jeanie drafted foundations for her diminutive Pine Tree blocks and used hand-dyed fabrics from Next Door Neighbor Dyeworks to achieve the "updated" look she desired.*

Materials

- 1 yard dark blue
- Light blue at least 7" square
- Fat quarter (18" x 20") each turquoise, light yellow, green, coral, and hot pink
- Purple at least 10" square
- 20" x 23" piece of backing fabric
- 20" x 23" piece of thin batting
- Paper for the foundations

Cutting

Fabric for foundation piecing will be cut as you stitch the foundations. Each piece should be at least 1/4" larger on all sides than the section it will cover. All other dimensions include a 1/4" seam allowance.

From the dark blue:
- Cut 3: 1 1/4" x 30" strips, for the binding
- Cut 4: 1 1/4" x 19" strips
- Cut 9: 2 3/8" squares
- Cut 3: 4" squares, then cut them in quarters diagonally to yield 12 setting triangles. You will use 9.
- Cut 2: 2 1/4" squares, then cut them in half diagonally to yield 4 corner triangles
- Cut 5: 1 1/4" x 11" strips
- Cut 8: 1" x 11" strips

From the light blue:
- Cut 2: 1 1/4" x 11" strips
- Cut 2: 1" x 11" strips

From the light yellow:
- Cut 2: 2 3/8" squares
- Cut 1: 4" square, then cut it in quarters diagonally to yield 4 setting triangles

- Cut 2: 1 1/4" x 11" strips

From the green:
- Cut 5: 2 3/8" squares
- Cut 1: 4" square, then cut it in quarters diagonally to yield 4 setting triangles. You will use 2.
- Cut 1: 1 1/4" x 11" strip

From the coral:
- Cut 5: 2 3/8" squares
- Cut 1: 4" square, then cut it in quarters diagonally to yield 4 setting triangles. You will use 2.
- Cut 1: 1" x 11" strip

From the hot pink:
- Cut 2: 1 1/4" x 11" strips
- Cut 1: 1" x 11" strip

Directions

The foundation patterns (page 25) are full size and do not include a seam allowance. Follow the foundation-piecing instructions in the General Directions *to piece the blocks.*

1. Trace the patterns on foundation paper, transferring all lines and numbers. Cut each one out on the outer line. Make 30 each of foundations A, B, and C. Make 60

foundation D's. For each block you will piece one each of foundations A, B, and C and 2 of foundation D.

2. Piece the foundations in numerical order using the colors indicated.

For one Foundation A:
- 1 - light yellow
- 2, 3 - dark blue
- 4 - light yellow

For one each of Foundations B and C:
- Odd numbers - dark blue
- Even numbers - light yellow

For 2 Foundation D's:
- Odd numbers - light yellow
- Even numbers - dark blue

3. Trim the fabric 1/4" beyond the edges of the foundations.

4. Stitch the two D foundations together, as shown. Stitch the B and C foundations together.

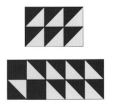

5. Stitch the 3 sections together to

make a block. Make one more block using light yellow for the tree and dark blue for the background.

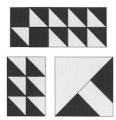

6. Make 4 blocks using coral for the trees and light yellow for the background.

7. Make 6 blocks using green for the trees and coral for the background.

8. Make 6 blocks using turquoise for the trees and green for the background.

9. Make 6 blocks using hot pink for the trees and dark blue for the background.

10. Make 4 blocks using purple for the trees and dark blue for the background.

11. Make 2 blocks using light blue for the trees and dark blue for the background.

For the border sections:

1. Using the 11"-long strips, stitch a 1" dark blue strip to a 1 1/4" light blue strip. Make 2.

2. Stitch a 1" light blue strip to a 1 1/4" dark blue strip. Make 2.

3. Stitch a 1" dark blue strip to a 1 1/4" light yellow strip. Make 2.

4. Stitch a 1" coral strip to a 1 1/4" dark blue strip.

5. Stitch a 1" dark blue strip to a 1 1/4" green strip.

6. Stitch a 1" dark blue strip to a 1 1/4" hot pink strip. Make 2.

7. Stitch a 1" hot pink strip to a 1 1/4" dark blue strip.

8. Stitch a 1" dark blue strip to a 1 1/4" dark blue strip. Set this pieced strip aside.

9. Press the seam allowance of each pieced strip toward the darker side. Cut each pieced strip (except the blue one) into two 5 1/2" sections.

Assembly

1. Lay out 4 hot pink tree blocks, the purple tree blocks, the light blue/dark blue tree blocks, and 3 dark blue setting triangles. Stitch them into diagonal rows and join the rows, as shown.

2. Center and stitch the 11"-long dark blue strip section to the tree section, placing the narrow strip against the tree section. Trim the ends of the strip even with the edges of the tree blocks. Be sure to leave a seam allowance.

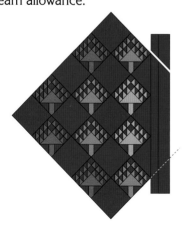

3. Stitch a dark blue setting triangle to a hot pink tree block. Stitch a hot pink/dark blue strip to the triangle, as shown. Carefully trim the strip even with the tree unit.

4. Make a hot pink tree unit, changing the angle, as shown.

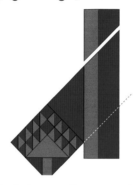

5. Stitch the small units to the larger tree unit.

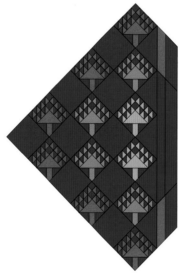

6. Center and stitch a dark blue corner triangle to a dark blue/hot pink strip. Stop stitching at the 1/4" seam allowance of the right angle corner and backstitch. Stitch a second dark

blue/hot pink strip to the triangle in the same manner.

7. Miter the corner. Trim the strips even with the triangle to make a corner unit, as shown. Make 2.

8. Stitch the corner units to the tree section, aligning the dark blue triangles with the tree blocks. Trim the left edge of each corner unit even with the tree section.

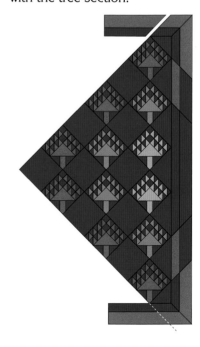

9. Lay out 3 turquoise/green tree blocks, two 2 3/8" green squares, and a green triangle. Join them to make a row. Stitch a dark blue/green strip section to the top of the row. Trim the ends even with the row. Stitch this section to the top left side of the tree section.

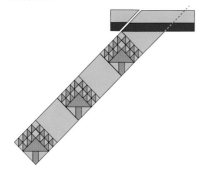

10. Refer to the Assembly Diagram for this step and the following steps. Lay out 3 turquoise/green tree blocks, three 2 3/8" green squares, and a green triangle. Join them to make a row. Stitch the remaining

dark blue/green strip section to the row and trim the ends. Stitch this section to the lower left side of the tree section.

11. Join 3 green/coral tree blocks, two 2 3/8" coral squares, and a coral triangle. Join them to make a row. Stitch a coral/dark blue strip section to the row and trim the ends. Stitch this row to the top left side of the tree section.

12. Lay out 3 green/coral tree blocks, three 2 3/8" coral squares, and a coral triangle. Join them to make a row. Stitch a coral/dark blue strip section to the row and trim the ends. Stitch this section to the lower left side of the tree section.

13. Make 2 rows each using 2 coral/light yellow tree blocks, a 2 3/8" light yellow square, and 2 light

yellow triangles. Stitch dark blue/light yellow strip sections to the rows and trim the ends. Sew them to the tree section.

14. Make 2 rows each using a light yellow/dark blue tree block and 2 dark blue setting triangles. Stitch light blue/dark blue strip sections to the rows and trim the ends. Sew them to the tree section.

15. Make 2 corner units as described in Steps 6 and 7, using dark blue corner triangles and dark blue/light blue strip sections. Sew them to the corners of the quilt.

16. Measure the length of the quilt. Trim 2 of the 1 1/4" x 19" dark blue strips to that measurement. Stitch them to the sides of the quilt.

17. Measure the width of the quilt, including the borders. Trim the remaining 1 1/4" x 19" dark blue strips to that measurement and stitch them to the top and bottom of the quilt.

18. Finish the quilt as described in the *General Directions*, using the 1 1/4" x 30" dark blue strips for the binding.

Assembly Diagram

Foundation B

1	3	5	7	9
2	4	6	8	

Foundation C

1	3	5	7	8
2	4	6		9

Foundation A

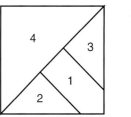

Materials

- Assorted scraps for the houses, trees, and grass
- 1/3 yard light blue for the background
- 1/4 yard blue print
- 21" square of backing fabric
- 21" square of thin batting
- Paper for the foundations

Little Houses

Edna Morse of Yuma, Arizona, made the **"Little Houses"** quilt. She learned how to design 6" "funky" houses in a class with designer Joanne Myers at the annual quilt show in Sisters, Oregon. She then went on to draft her own 3" houses and added trees, an airplane, and a sailboat to complete the landscape.

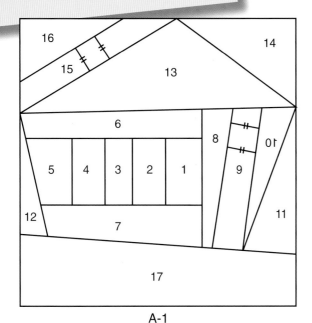

A-1

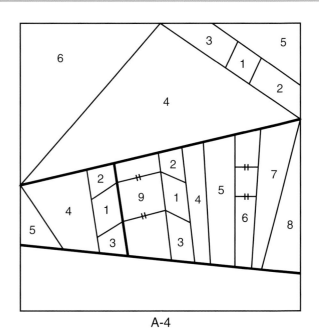

A-4

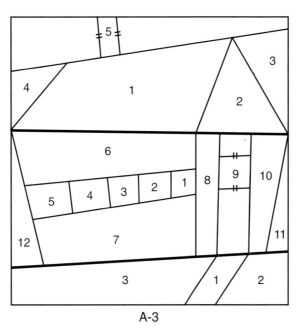

A-2

A-3

Cutting

Fabric for foundation piecing will be cut as you stitch the blocks. Each piece should be at least 1/4" larger on all sides than the section it will cover. Refer to the **General Directions** as needed. All other dimensions include a 1/4" seam allowance.

- Cut 2: 2" x 19" strips, blue print, for the border
- Cut 2: 2" x 16" strips, blue print, for the border
- Cut 4: 1 1/4" x 20" strips, blue print, for the binding

Directions

The foundation patterns are full size and do not include a seam allowance. Follow the foundation-piecing instructions in the General Directons *to piece the foundations.*

1. The foundation patterns are labeled by row and position. For example: A-2 indicates row A, block 2. Some blocks are divided into several sections as indicated by bold lines. Trace the patterns, transferring all lines and numbers. Cut the foundations on the bold lines for blocks with multiple sections.

2. Working on one block at a time, piece each foundation in numerical order. Use assorted scraps for the houses, trees, and grass and light blue for the background. Sections marked with small double slash marks should be pre-sewn before stitching those sections to the foundation.

3. For unmarked sections such as the grass in block A-4, assemble the pieced foundations then add that section. Add a piece that is larger than necessary, then trim the block to 3 1/2" square.

4. Join the sections for each block.

Assembly

1. Lay out the foundations in order in 5 rows.

2. Stitch the blocks into rows. Join the rows.

3. Measure the length of the quilt.

Trim the 2" x 16" blue print strips to that measurement. Stitch them to the sides of the quilt.

4. Measure the width of the quilt, including the borders. Trim the 2" x 19" blue print strips to that measurement. Stitch them to the top and bottom of the quilt.

5. Finish the quilt as described in the *General Directions*, using the 1 1/4 x 20" blue print strips and binding method #2.

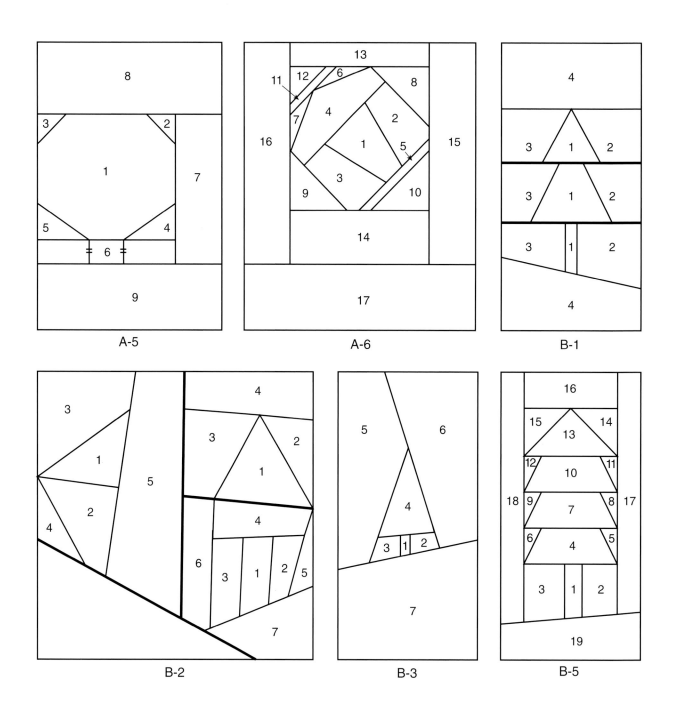

A-5

A-6

B-1

B-2

B-3

B-5

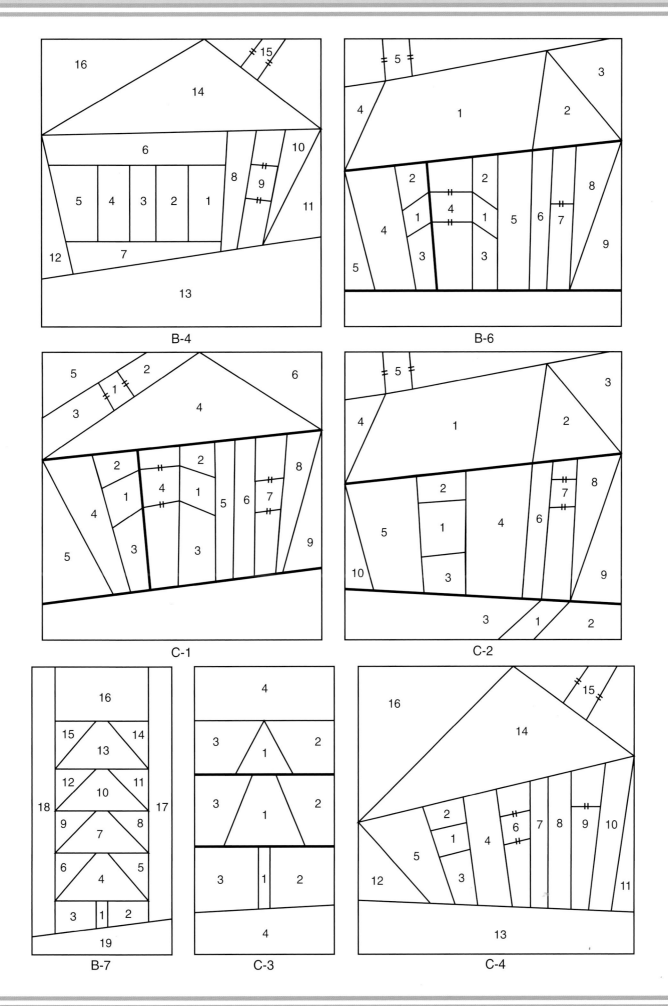

B-4

B-6

C-1

C-2

B-7

C-3

C-4

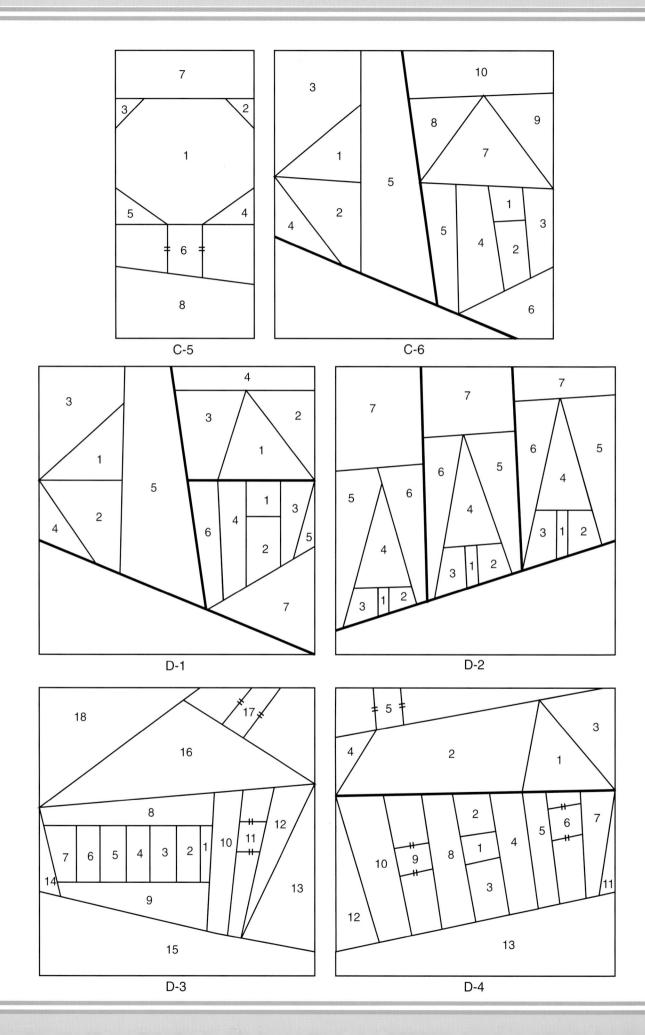

C-5

C-6

D-1

D-2

D-3

D-4

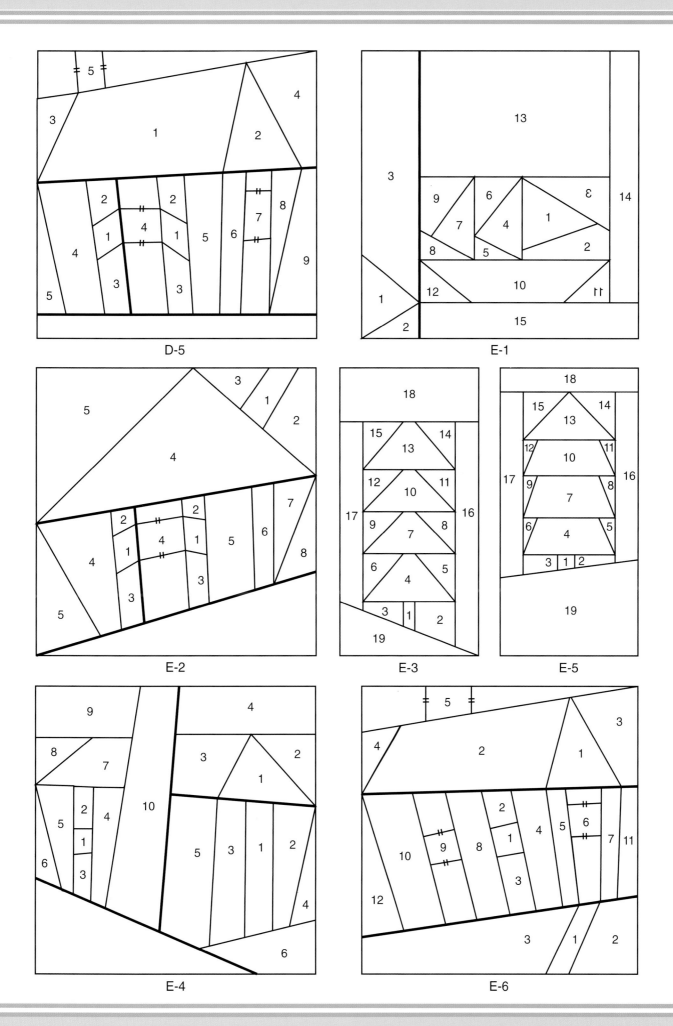

D-5

E-1

E-2

E-3

E-5

E-4

E-6

General Directions

About the Patterns

Read through the pattern directions before cutting fabric for the quilt.

Fabrics

Yardage is based on fabric with a useable width of 40". We recommend using 100% cotton fabrics. We suggest washing your fabrics before using them.

Marking Fabric

Always test marking tools for removability. We suggest using silver or white marking tools for dark fabrics and fine-line pencils for light fabrics.

Templates

Template patterns are full size and, unless otherwise noted, include a 1/4" seam allowance. Trace patterns on clear plastic.

Pieced Patterns

For machine piecing, make templates with the seam allowance. Trace around the templates on the right side of the fabric. For hand piecing, make templates without the seam allowance. Trace templates on the wrong side of the fabric, flipping all directional (asymmetrical) templates before tracing, and add a 1/4" seam allowance as you cut the fabric pieces out.

Foundation-pieced Patterns

Place fabric pieces on the unmarked side of the foundation and stitch on the marked side. Center the first piece, right side up, over position 1 on the unmarked side of the foundation. Hold the foundation up to a light to make sure that the raw edges of the fabric extend at least 1/2" beyond the seamline on all sides. Hold this first piece in place with a small dab of glue or a pin, if desired. Place the fabric for position 2 on the first piece, right sides together. Turn the foundation over and sew on the line between 1 and 2, extending the stitching past the beginning and end of the line by a few stitches on both ends. Trim the seam allowance to 1/8". Fold the position 2 piece back, right side up, and press. Continue adding pieces to the foundation in the same manner until all positions are covered and the block is complete. Trim the fabric 1/4" beyond the edges of each foundation.

To avoid disturbing the stitches, do not remove the paper until the blocks have been stitched together and the borders have been added, unless instructed to remove them sooner in the pattern. The pieces will be perforated from the stitching and can be gently pulled free. Use tweezers to carefully remove small sections of the paper, if necessary.

Machine Sewing

Set the stitch length to 12 stitches per inch. Stitch pieces together from edge to edge unless directed to do otherwise in the pattern. When directions call for you to start or stop stitching 1/4" from the edges, as for set-in pieces, backstitch to secure the seam.

FINISHING

Marking Quilting Designs

Simple designs can be cut from adhesive-backed shelf paper. They'll stick and re-stick several times. Masking tape can be used to mark grids. Remove the tape when you're not quilting to avoid leaving a sticky residue. Mark lightly with pencils; thick lines that won't go away really stand out on a small quilt.

Batting

Use a thin batting. Layer the quilt sandwich as follows: backing, wrong side up, batting; quilt top, right side up. Baste or pin the layers together.

Quilting

Very small quilts can be lap-quilted without a hoop. Larger ones can be quilted in a hoop or small frame. Use a short, thin needle (between) and small stitches that will be in scale with the little quilt. Thread the needle with a single strand of thread and knot one end. Insert the needle through the quilt top and batting (not the backing) 1/2" away from where you want to begin quilting. Gently pull the thread to pop the knot through the top and bury it in the batting. Quilt as desired.

Binding–Method #1

For most straight-edged quilts, a double-fold French binding is an attractive, durable and easy finish. NOTE: *If your quilt has curved or scalloped edges, binding strips must be cut on the bias of the fabric. Sew the binding strips together with diagonal seams; trim and press the seams open.*

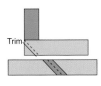

Trim one end of the strip at a 45º angle. Press one long edge of the binding strip 1/4" toward the wrong side. Starting with the trimmed end, position the binding strip, right sides together, on the quilt top, aligning the raw edge of the binding with the bottom edge of the quilt top. Leaving approximately 2" of the binding strip free, and beginning at least 3 inches from one corner, stitch the binding to the bottom of the quilt with a 1/4" seam allowance, measuring from the edge of the binding and quilt top.

When you reach a corner, stop the stitching line exactly 1/4" from the edge of the quilt top.

Backstitch, clip threads, and remove the quilt from the machine. Fold the binding up and away, creating a 45º angle, as shown.

Fold the binding down as shown, and begin stitching at the edge.

Continue stitching around the quilt to within 2" of the starting point. Lay the binding flat against the quilt, overlapping the beginning end. Open the pressed edge on each end and fold the end of the binding at a 45º angle against the angle on the beginning end of the binding. Finger press the fold.

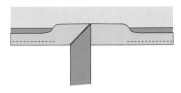

Trim 1/2" beyond the fold line. Place the ends of the binding right sides together and stitch with a 1/4" seam allowance. Finger press the seam allowance open.

Place the binding flat against the quilt and finish stitching it to the quilt. Trim the batting and backing even with the edge of the quilt top. Fold the binding over the edge of the quilt, and blindstitch the folded edge to back, covering the seamline.

Binding–Method #2

Cut 4 binding strips as directed in the pattern. Press one long edge of each binding strip 1/4" toward the wrong side. Center a pressed strip to the quilt with a 1/4" seam allowance. Trim the binding ends even with the edge of the quilt.

Trim the backing and batting even with the edge of the quilt along that side. Fold the binding over the edge of the quilt and blindstitch the folded edge to the back, covering the seamline. Repeat for the opposite side of the quilt.

Center and stitch a pressed strip to one remaining side of the quilt. Trim the ends of the strip 1/4" beyond the edge of the quilt top.

Trim the backing and batting even with the edge of the quilt top. Fold the ends of the binding strip 1/4" toward the wrong side. Fold the binding toward the back, as before, and blindstitch it to the back of the quilt. Stitch the ends closed. Repeat for the remaining side of the quilt.